I Found my Heart

Stacie Ann Green-Taylor

Published by Stacie Ann Green-Taylor & Pete Taylor

Print ISBN 978-976-96575-0-2

eBook ISBN 978-976-96575-1-9

Dedication

This book is for every woman who has encountered disappointment, endured pain, lived through overwhelming circumstances and found the courage to triumph. You are my mother, my sister, my friend, my heroine. You inspire me to cherish this journey.

Contents

TROUVAILLE

Introduction

I Found my Heart is a story that speaks of a woman's journey through varying seasons of her life. The story, expressed in the form of prose and poetry, takes the reader into the crevices of the author's heart. It delves into her encounters with disappointment, explores the journey of finding courage through self-discovery and provides invaluable perspectives on the human experience.

I Found my Heart speaks about challenging issues that confront us daily yet for a multiplicity of reasons we remain muted. It speaks for many women who are intimidated by their circumstances and are afraid of the discomfort others may feel when the truth is spoken. It vividly describes what is seen, heard and felt in the author's innermost being during her worst and best days.

This is a story of acceptance, forgiveness and intentional actions that lead to self-discovery. It provides insight into the revolutionizing force of courage and shows the importance of understanding and accepting one's true purpose.

I Found my Heart is significant because it is an authentic story told about the human experience. Its aim is to inspire women to use every trial as a tool; a tool that can be used to fuel purpose and rise above it all hence finding their heart.

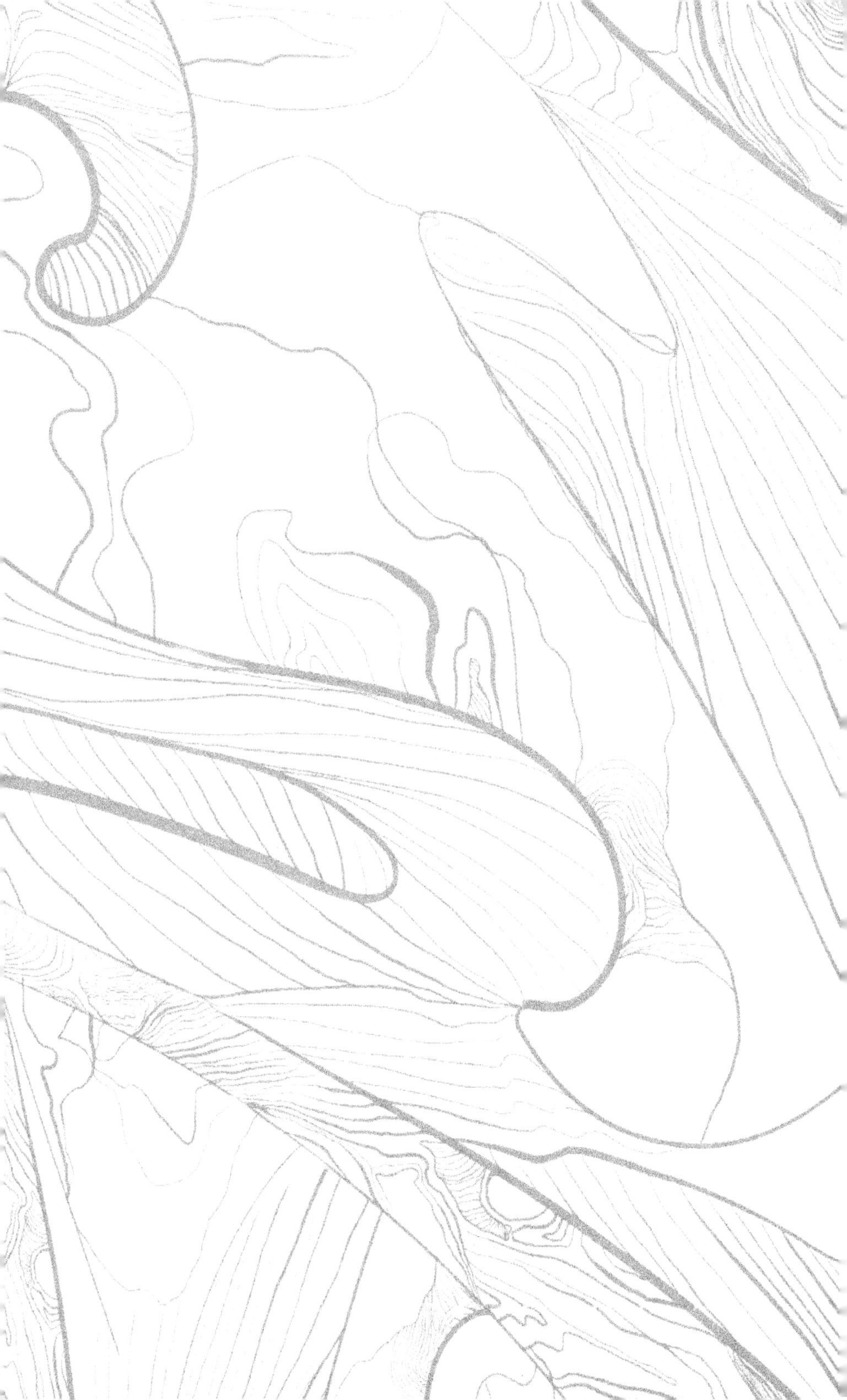

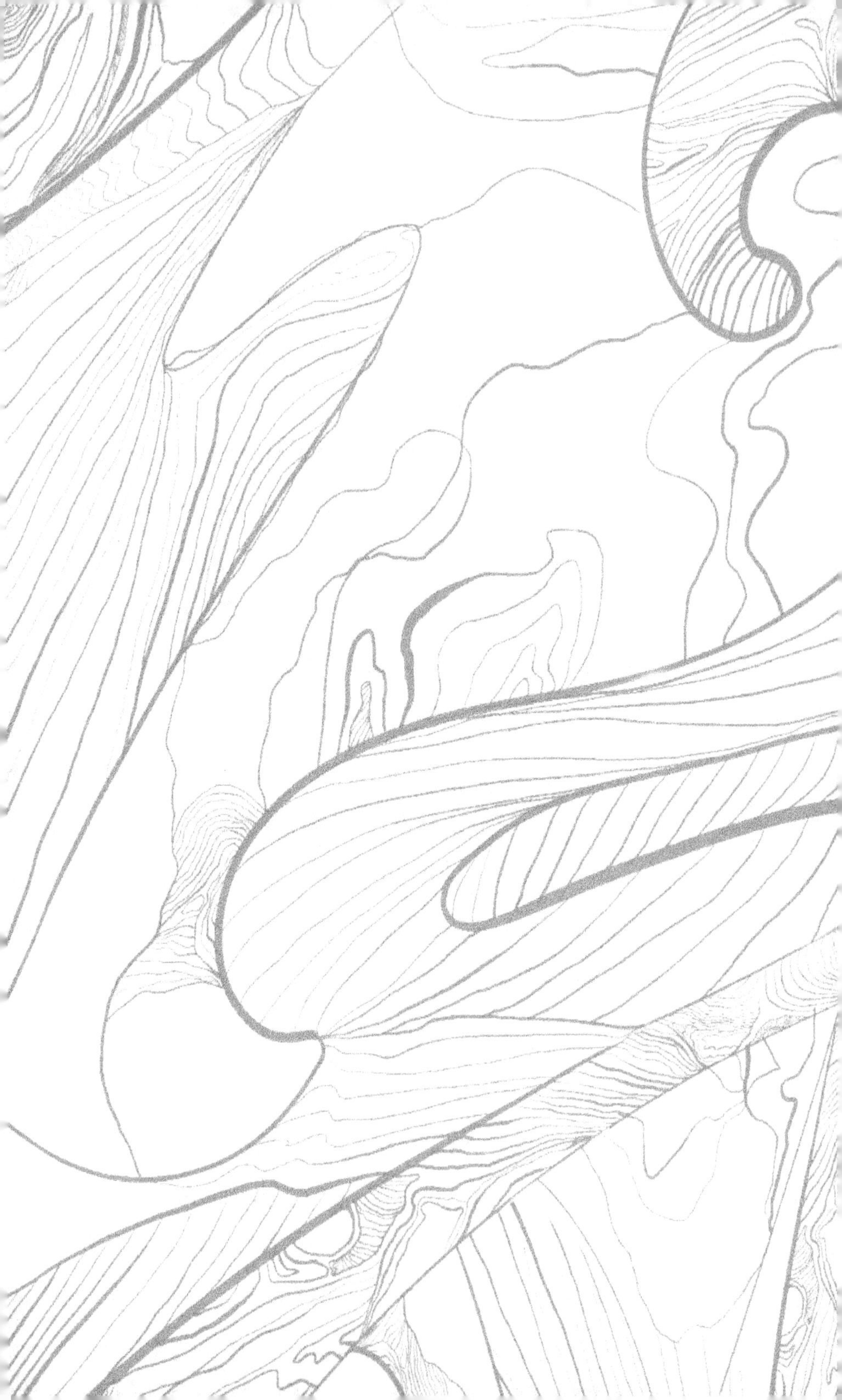

On days when her silence scares her, she knows it is time
to write.

FINITE DISAPPOINTMENTS

The end

8

Love eluded,

betrayed,

empty,

scarred she walked away.

Silent liar

Lies grinning through silence,
deafening truths,
she refused to admit,
believing a made-up love story,
silence screaming,
she refused to quit.

Friendship sought,
that to him unknown,
lying more with silence
than he ever did with words.

In time
it will be learnt
never to seek love
from a duplicitous man.

Table for three

Beautiful fairy-tale
all planned in my dreams;
as it turns out
it was a table for three.

Fascinated by expectations,
naivety's slave,
committed to a master
of lies and deceit.

Perfect triangle,
love never part of the dream,
my share was never enough
sitting at a table for three.

Chaotic memories

Thwarted plans,
insurmountable fear,
incurable grief,
betrayal's hostage,
pain no relief.

Trepidations
carefully tucked
beneath my sleeves.
Glimpses of my vision
only black and white I see.

Severed spirit
entrapped in chaotic memories,
perfect tribute
to my plight.

Stranger

Seeking silence,

solace,

serenity and peace.

Heaving heart,

sobbing soul,

grief,

shadows

and empty hallways.

Once again,

I am a stranger

to my soul.

Heart of winter

13

She was selfish with her pain,
burdened by her plight yet,
she kept that smile
like evergreen trees
in the heart of winter.

I found my heart

I lost my heart to the surgeon's plunge,

it was damaged,

bleeding,

barely beating.

I found my heart in the surgeon's bin,

no hope of survival,

utterly broken,

no chance of healing.

I found my heart in the scavenger's heap,

rejected and pale

from whence ravaging

left me limp.

I found my heart in the trenches of despair;

snakes and scorpions were its company,

their sweet venom

a welcome sedative to my pain.

I found my heart

washed up on the shore,

cold,

shrivelled,

lifeless almost,

it was floating adrift for days

among the tumultuous waves.

I found my heart in the graveyard

among the tombs,

buried beneath rotting bodies,

no chance

of being exhumed.

Notebook

16

Invisible teacher,

how do I take notes?

My frigid fingers quiver,

every plan fallen out of place.

Apology

Her mind retold the story
she tried to soothe the ache,
eager to forgive
she kept her heart open
to the innocent culprit.

I apologize to my soul
for refusing to be free,
I apologize to my soul
for begging for love in places
I was never meant to be.

Did I earn these wages fairly?
Did my decision to love put me in this pain?
A mask for a crown a circus called home.

Mirror secrets part 1

A stranger's blank gaze greets me,
my reflection,
fragile layers unfolding,
falling fast at my feet.

Shreds,
eyes empty from the reign of bitter tears,
lost recollections of love,
solitude has taken wings again.

Dust filled eyes,
stinging teardrops,
alone her head hangs.

Mirror secrets part 2

Considering the bizarre
my face stares back at me.

Am I a weirdo,
some morbid epiphany of my own dreams?
Am I a reflection of my own conscience?
Is my conscience a reflection of me?

In contemplating the bizarre
my face stares back at me.

Trenches

Cowering in the trenches,
head between my legs,
mind wide open,
eyes closed in dread.

Politeness disregarded,
labelled a fool,
treasured tactics have failed me,
so has the golden rule.

Pretence charged and loaded,
expelled at my feet,
like mortar they explode
leaving me bruised and beat.

The stench of ignorance rises,
its fumes bottled like expensive perfume.
My emotions collateral damage,
have I no defence?
While cruelty ensnares me,
I turn the other cheek.

Charging into winter

Charging into winter,
out in the open without a coat.

I am unprepared for this spell,
my only comrade a boat.

Like a squirrel
displaced I must make haste,
the predators are out.

Every green leaf unexpectedly withered,
winter itself rebels.

Treasured nuts apprehended and stored;
carpeted leaves gone
MY MIDDEN DOOR!

Unforgiving winter what else do you have in store?

Anaesthesia

Beautiful Anaesthesia make haste,
release me from the clutches of this hysteria.

Relieve my agony
meditation affords no escape.
Anaesthesia are you awake?

Anaesthesia be my saviour
or I will be lost forever all options fled.

Don't close your ears to my plea,
one dose will be sufficient.
Will I have to go on my knees?

Anaesthesia just this once
hear my cry I cannot run;
the absence of you will be my only demise.

Anaesthesia open the gate.

I need you,

how long must I wait?

Is this plague here to stay?

Anaesthesia one last time,

have you abandoned me for the night?

Anaesthesia gently close these eyes.

Shifting clouds

24

All shutters down
awaiting the deluge
but ah it's just shifting clouds.

My smile just died,
shadows pounce
I stand wide eyed,
my heart thumps
attuned to the pace of the sinking sun.

The heat of the day has been broken.
Vibrations of thunder
finally put my mind at ease
but would you believe
it was only shifting clouds.

Rugged road

25

Where the rugged road leads
life kicked her in the knees,
the extra mile was conquered slow.

Deserving a new beginning
the path narrows close to healing,
this painful journey
I must continue alone.

When

The journey will begin
when she catches her breath again
but when?

She hobbles to her knees
no strength in her feet
but when?

She hopes for sunshine days
she refuses to remain a slave
but when?

Hope denied,
the caterpillar folded and died
again.

The game has been played,
she counts her losses once again,
no chance to score she waits.

Let me be

27

And today just let me be,
I have nurtured caterpillars,
the butterflies all
flew away from me.

Broken spirit

She is losing patience.
Her faith is shaken.
Her heart faints,
she cries in silence.

She is writhing in pain.
Her heart cries out,
she needs healing.

She cannot utter words.
She can only groan.
Her spirit is broken.

Honey

Just a drop of honey
to take this bitter taste away.
A drop of honey
and I'll be on my way.

Just a drop of honey
to give me peace of mind.
A drop of honey
to take this bitter taste away.

Incomplete

Why deny the reality we exist in?
Too terrified to shatter the glass ceiling?

Hiding from the truth
that stares us in the face
without accepting
it is much too harsh to embrace.

We hate with unbiased passion
while our inherent jealousy cannot be rationed.

We love without feeling
because our hearts do not know the true meaning.

We possess eyes yet,
we cannot see
being too blind to our true reality.

Again

Today I made a move
to start loving me again,
it was painfully frightening
excruciating even.

I gazed into the mirror
my face was stone cold,
in an attempt to conceal scars,
I was directed to my soul.

My soul was calloused
from the pain and loss;
I had nothing there to love
just a wealth of misery.

I searched for warmth,
a little sunshine,
it was nowhere to be found.
I screamed in anguish
all this time
I was a clown.

Renaissance

32

She knew the story
had to change;
she started listening
to her own advice.

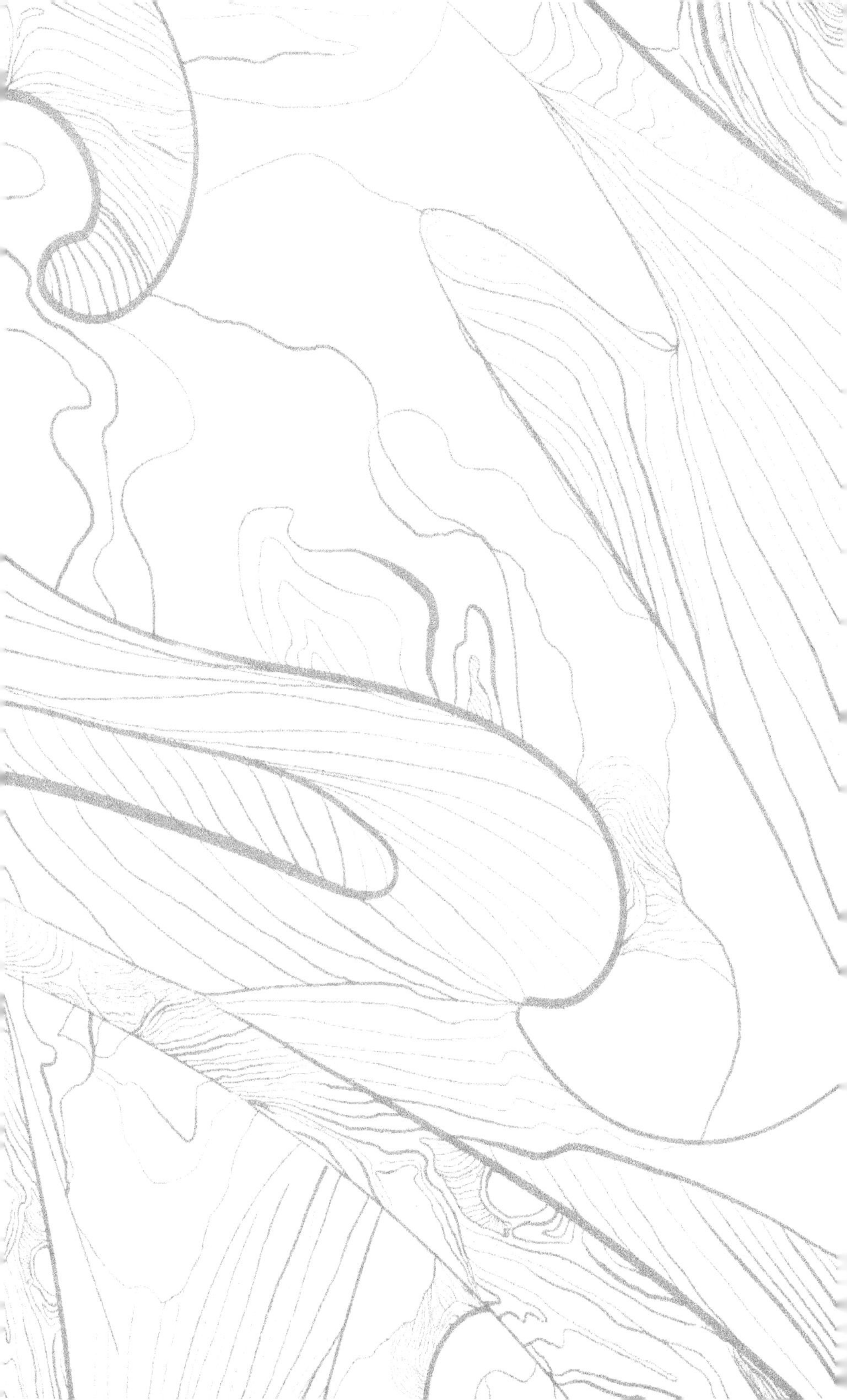

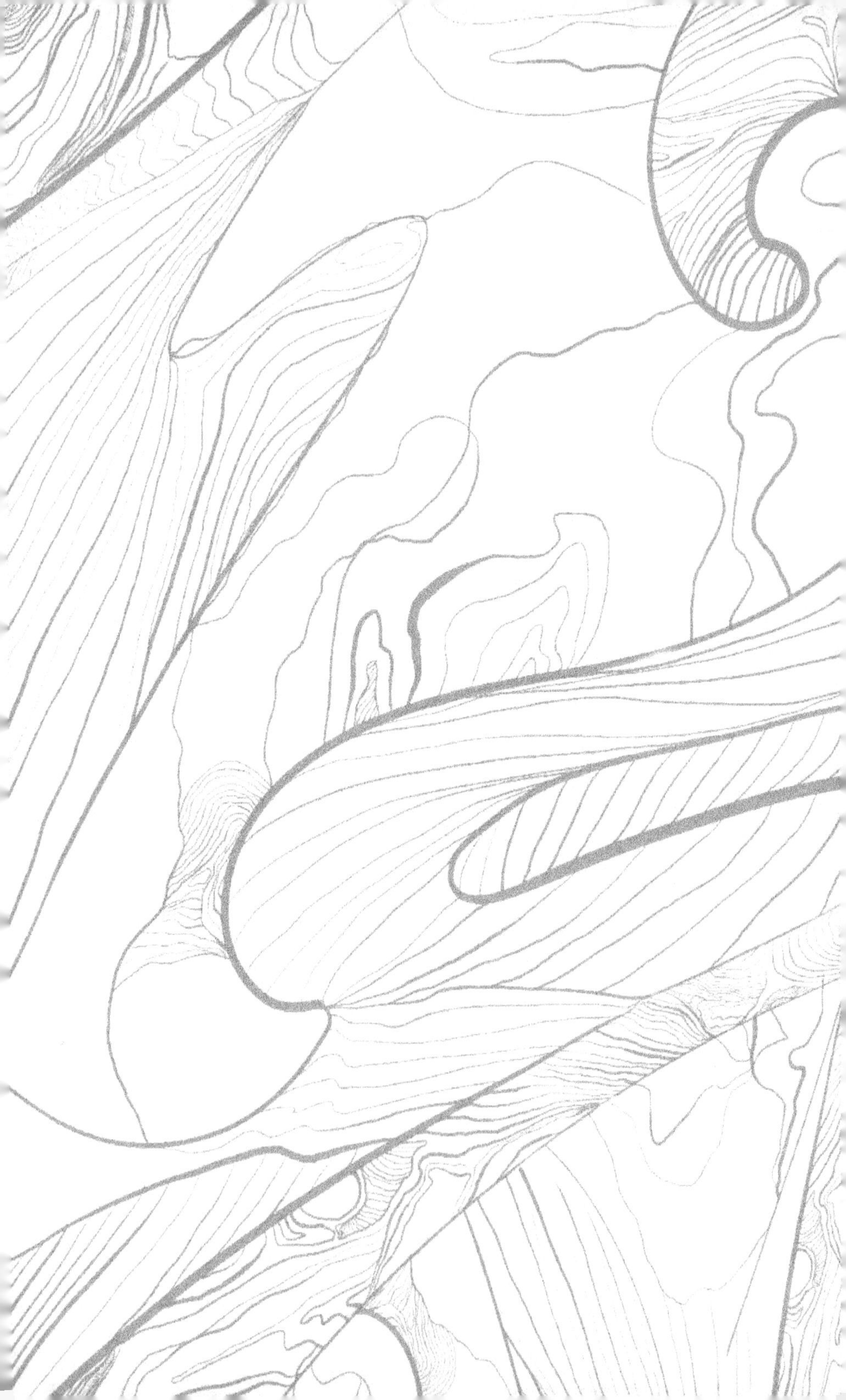

And today again I write, something new has awakened inside.

Today I write the things I choose not to speak; they are many and varied all simple intricacies.

I write above the noise many hear but never listen.

Today they will understand.

SUMMONED COURAGE

Golden cage

She will conquer her fears

when she makes a move,

the moment she exits

the golden cage.

I am not listening

I hear voices speaking loudly,
impressive speeches,
concerned tones
but one thing I am sure of,
I will not listen
I trust my soul.

There was a time
I would have listened
but that faded with the night,
I see beyond the cloaked laughter,
I see beyond the masks.

I hear voices but
I refuse to listen,
the roof collapsed and I know.

You wonder why I am indifferent;
I can hear you
even when your voice is low.

I hear you
but I refuse to listen,
you can speak in angelic tones.

Your words hold no meaning,
I listen with my eyes
I bet you did not know.

This I know

41

There are those who will talk at you, others will talk about you, some will talk around you, engage only those who are sincere enough to speak with you.

I will speak

I will speak,
my heart has been silent for too long.
My side of the story
always told and I,
an uninvited guest
to its audition.

I will speak,
I will not consider the discomfort
others may feel at my utterances.
I have lived long enough
with the whisperings
and pointed fingers
of the crowd.

I will speak,
I will not use hushed tones.
Let the guilty face this story,
my side was never told.

I will speak,

this time my voice will not quiver;

it has been summoned

by a thousand thunders

that for years let me shake.

I will speak and the caves of silence will echo;

they hold stories of change

the spirits are now awake.

I will speak,

not a word will be left

shrouded in the tombs.

The womb of time

has birthed a new day

in time for the new moon.

I will speak,

I will not be silenced;

my words will roam

the streets in garments of jubilee.

I will speak,

I cannot be silenced with shame.

The secret of my peace sings a new song,

the orchestra makes its way.

I miss you not

Late night stalker at this very hour!
I miss you?
How do I avenge
the memory of this weakling
when I found a way to love me more?

Late night stalker be gone!
In times past
you would have succeeded
in robbing me of my dreams;
I marvel at this piece of chaotic history.

No warmth in my heart
on this cold rainy night,
cut the stage lights
the lightening a cue.

Can we be friends?

Heard this line before,
a deceiver's attempt
to find a door
back to the heart
of the desperate broken soul.

It's a question you don't answer then,
action is the best defence
against the manipulator's plot.

It was carefully thought out;
heartbreakers know you are in doubt
and prey on moments of weakness
like a snake.

It's a grand masquerade,
refuse don't hesitate,
those words must die a swift cold death.
No need to be a fool's fool no more.

Walk

Yesterday
I walked those
dark, lonely,
cobblestone roads
barefooted and alone.

Yesterday
I mourned you
in loud wailing tones
but today I rise
with the sun in my face.

I smile
each time
a beautiful tear reveals the truth
in my heart.

White flag

She refuses
to let her guard down;
she tightens the chains
around her fragile heart.

Fear bursting
through her soul,
flood waters rising,
damned.

Emotions emerge
like an angry bull
chasing the fighter
around the ring.

She heads for the safety
of the walled alleys
worn out from the fights
she did not win.

She exchanges the red flags

for white ones,

she knows

it will be an uphill task.

Her heart

has brought her to this place,

she intends

never to look back.

Pity party

Fabulous pity party!
Is the sun up today?
We cannot see its beauty
the clouds present its shade.

Nature can be mischievous,
wake up,
clap back,
take a cue.
I see the heavens are open
it may rain on your parade too.

Those tears you shed
in the sunshine,
would they be welcome today?

No need
to get the umbrella,
step out and face the day.

Storm clouds never

intimidate the sun,

what is your excuse?

Venting pen

Today's epiphany
my golden venting pen,
it has spared me many verbal conflicts,
my book its victim
like prey thrown in the lion's den.

My pen is swift and ruthless,
giving no thought
to its iron clad words;
it speaks with riveting emotion
healing every painful scar.

Its venting relieves every sorrow,
pages riddled
with bullet proof truths,
lessons of deception and heartbreak,
days
when rainbows were blue.

My venting pen

meanders through dark hallways,

trots down footpaths

that left me bruised,

easing the pain

that held me hostage.

My golden venting pen

reveals the truth.

If I had the chance

Dear Karma,

unbelievable revenge,

could I relish in your magic?

Autograph his heart

with my venting pen?

Let me rehearse

this toxic tribute,

let me gloat

in this charade,

I waited patiently for this moment,

my friend Karma

you are welcome to stay.

Let me take sincere words for granted,

reintroduce

some brutal truths,

offer excuses for commitment,

conjure sweet lies

reward this brute.

My eyes are now wide open,
callousness flows through these veins,
not an ounce of compassion wasted,
anger pouring through like rain.

Dark secrets naked,
splattered against the wall of shame.

Unmuted
Dear Karma,
don't let me wait in vain.

Open rebellion

Excellence is open rebellion to the mediocre mind. Incompetence fears brilliance, there is very little room for compromise when both meet.

Nurturers of mediocrity

Billowing clouds of mediocrity
hang high;
clouded visions
parading in their golden cloak.

Nurturers of mediocrity
proudly celebrating
while dark crevices cry out.

The stakes are high
for the mediocre mind,
not an ounce
of his weakness
must give way to growth.

Excellence challenged,
he dares not raise his ugly head,
quick rebuke or else he will be exposed.

Entrapped in his bubble

the cycle continues;

he marches on

humming his own comforting songs.

Such travesty my heart weeps.

Diamonds of pomposity

Kindness wrapped

in sparkly sandpaper gold;

sweet words dipped in gall

on the serpent's tongue.

Razor sharp grins

packaged as smiles;

the brick wall leans

transparent on my side.

Broken humans

who have lost touch with their souls,

labelling antics as friendship

attempting to break the strong

to feel whole.

Subliminal messages labelled as jokes,

knife in my back,

fool's gold at my throat.

Unbridled commendation,
bought with Judas' silver.
My guilty pleasure,
a clown's rehearsal
imitating the clever.

Remember

We can learn
to appreciate Judas
when he is not our friend;
do not seek to inherit him.

Do not seek
to establish bonds
with scorpions and snakes,
their intent is always the same.

Never share your burden
with the scoffer,
your pain
will be multiplied,
simply starve him of truths,
he will make
perfectly miscalculated moves.
His motives uncovered thrown out in the cold.

The critic's friend

I have met the critic's friend,
her name is incompetence,
she sees the flaws,
she knows it all,
from her tongue there is no escape.

The thing I never comprehend
is her lack of exceptional talents,
her most consistent trait pretence.

She never takes a break
admiring her self-exalting ways,
with her own ignorance
she is never appalled.

I have one question now
and when I ask
your head you must not bow.
Incompetence are you ready for the stage?

The uninspired

63

Be wary of the uninspired,

through his eyes

the world is a maze.

Your strength and resilience

convince him

that he is a coward,

it vexes him

to know you are brave.

Be wary of the uninspired,

in his eyes

your values are flaws.

Your hunger for your dreams

unnerves him,

you forever

bear the burden of being misread.

Be wary of the uninspired
and accept
his resentful gaze.
Your boundaries
to him make you a felon,
your passion
is ruthlessness he claims.

Be wary of the uninspired,
your confidence
he consistently hates,
not that it must be feared or lauded
he calls it arrogance night and day.

Be wary of the uninspired,
the world in his eyes is chaos,
an unwelcome reflection of a sin.
Remain undaunted by his accusations;
your journey may inspire others like him.

The cynic

The cynic strikes again,
executioner of dreams,
true believer of lies,
self-professed sage.

He never harbours doubt
about his invisible clout;
the party of enabling drunkards
cheers him on.

Some days I feel his pain,
compassion I think he has regained
but the cynic that he is,
he strikes again.

Do not

Woman your heart is golden,

your story is beautiful,

your testimony is powerful.

Do not be discouraged

by the opinion of the critic

who has never

felt the hot sand in your shoes.

Let them

On any given day in any given space your presence will either inspire or aggravate. Allow every man that freedom to choose.

Warrior

She has mastered the art of ignoring trash talk,

it no longer gets in her way,

she remains gracious

through the bitterness that is hurled,

it falls at her feet.

She has mastered the art of being calm,

there is no need for any human

to attempt to raise an argument for her.

She is a warrior and when words fail,

her character stands immovable.

Acceptance

Celebrate loudly and you will be
accused of being boastful.
Remain silent and you will be
accused of being selfish.

Those are labels
the cynic secretly wears
but feels more at ease
imposing them on you
when your light shines.

Embrace life with a grateful heart,
walk humbly,
honour your purpose,
celebrate your successes.

Strong

70

On your weakest day you can choose to be strong, it takes effort and courage.

Move on

There is no need to remain loyal

to a toxic human

who helped you through a rough season.

Pay your dues,

express your gratitude,

forgive,

accept peace,

move on.

She thrives

She does not process noise;

the fierceness in her eyes

is the fire she needs to thrive.

Life has knocked her down

a few times

but her purpose is higher

she will thrive.

On the other side

We have been flung
on the other side
of the train tracks;
daily we pass
the rising dumps of collective waste.

Our children play amongst cracked tombs.
Is this our lot
or is it a plan
to sell us a future that spells doom?

Their first canvas graffiti laden walls,
a collective diary of broken people
burdened
with unwritten stories.

No flower gardens
to soften our gaze,
the need to survive keeps us moving in haste.

On warm nights

we remain restless and pained

as our children fall asleep

to the hum

of the sewage plant's main.

Intertwined in its midst,

the low incessant mutterings of men,

now drunk with disappointment

speak of a life

that was once good.

I wonder about those on the other side,

I wonder if those who pass in the trains

are curious about us too.

We gaze with wonder

at their faces behind the train's dusty window;

oh, the beauty and grandeur

that must be on the other side.

They tell us if we work hard,
we will actually rise.
We dare to dream,
we dare to rise above the stench,
above the dry bones,
above the rhetoric
that we are to be blamed.

Should I really cross over these train tracks?
Find a dream they say,
you are worthy too.

For my children's sake
I will have to make it,
this side of the train track
has for too long been their school.

Empty spaces

I left empty spaces

in places once filled with pain;

in pursuit of peace,

I gave it all up

for a chance to new life.

The hand of the creator

rested firmly on me,

unsolicited

he awakened my soul.

I was restless

and burdened by pain,

I thought I was in control.

I left empty spaces inside,

and found my inheritance was free.

Who would have thought

that these empty spaces

would have given me such relief?

I walk around

with the empty spaces

never mind if I seem too at ease;

this place of peace

never came easy

I fought long and hard redeemed.

Aligned

With the passing of time
the pain of leaving it
all behind wanes.

Never envisioned feeling this way,
I see more sunshine
than skies of grey
I am sure.

My doubts marched out the door,
heart mended
right down to the core,
dancing over my pot of gold.

I lost my senses then,
wasted years in penitence,
used up tears
I could have saved
for this very hour.

This joy is divine,
my heart is full
it was all aligned.

Starfish

Be gentle with yourself,

learn from the starfish.

In time the wound will heal;

a new limb will grow again.

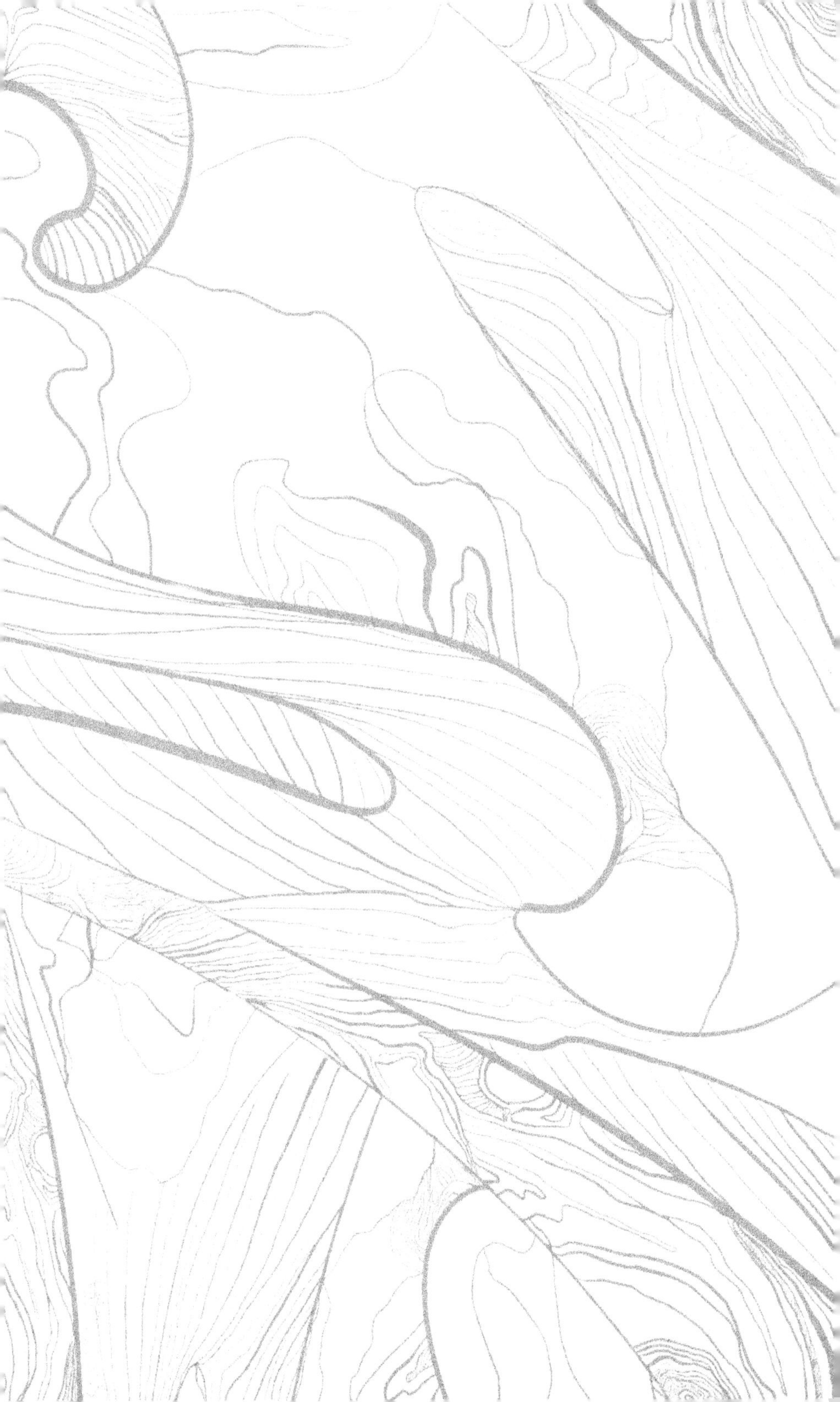

Each new season of your life will bring you treasures that cannot be stored.

TROUVAILLE

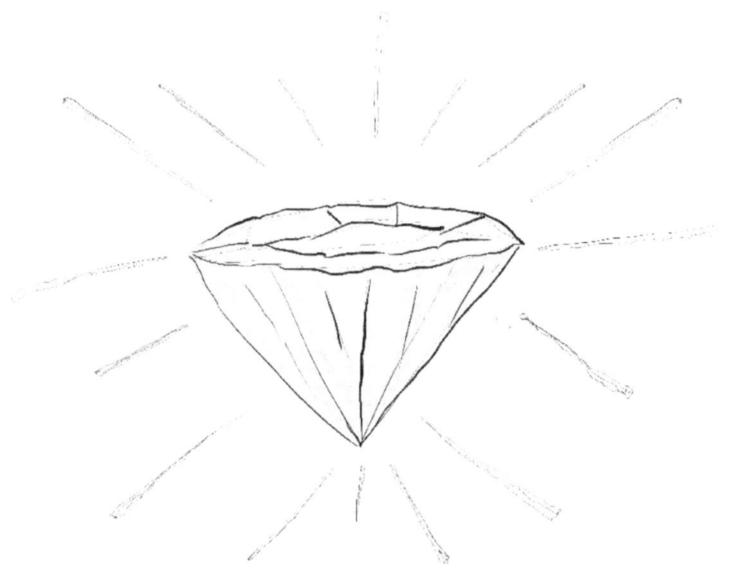

Fair exchange

Winter came and I buried them
at the root of the evergreen trees.

I smiled all the way to the burial,
moment of truth the eulogy.

Mourners lined the fields
in the colours of the rainbow,
heads unbowed
facing the sunshine welcoming spring.

I buried the cycles
a new season begins.

The river flows

The beauty of the journey
the traveller's vision dictates;
mountains of hope rise up
where storm clouds once loomed
threatening defeat.

Inspiration ignited,
channels of passion
through highs and lows.
Where purpose is nurtured
the rivers of progress will flow.

Where tears once flowed
rivers burst through
welcoming spring;
passion flows
like lava through the field.

With perpetual focus
fearless spirits cannot be broken
neither can courage be shaken.

Divine guidance eliminates
discouraging factions,
negativity
stands no chance to grow.

Boulders shudder,
imposters exposed,
purpose smiling broadly
amidst missiles of stone.

Like the river that flows
we go through highs and lows yet,
the river still flows.

It's coming

There are many lessons
some don't fully understand;
looking at another's blessings
thinking
their day will never come.

Each side of the mountain
gets its fair share of rain,
sometimes
at a different hour,
sometimes
a different day.

It may not rain on your side
of the mountain today
but it's coming.

The fog

They do not shrink
when they break the wind.

They do not tremble
or slump their shoulders
under the menacing
thunderstorm and rain.

Planted
by divine hands
the mountains
will remain undaunted,
though obscured
by the fleeting fog.

It's time to live again,
the fog lifts yet,
the mountains remain.

Silent witness

I am a silent witness,
purpose reigns in me;
my prayers all answered,
not one as I expected it to be.

In times of abundance,
ingratitude makes us weep
but days of scarcity prove
there is very little we need.

I never doubt that he laughs,
you know that oh too well.
I do not pray with words;
he sees and hears my thoughts.

My lips do not sing of redemption,
my heart is in constant commune.
I am a silent witness,
in sync with the phases of the moon.

Woman

She knows broken,
she nurtured it,
she knows wounded,
he was her friend,
she knows healing,
she had to become it.

The rebirth of woman
unbreakable spirit she flies high.

She is fire, hope,
passion and light,
she stands alive.

Choices

93

As you age you will realize that most people struggle with the same battles you face. The ones at peace are those who choose relevant battles to fight and many days you will realize they do not fight at all.

Time

94

Invest invaluable time improving yourself,

nurture your thoughts,

take care of your health,

water your gift,

get in touch with your soul.

Take the time to learn something new,

share in a cause greater than yourself,

it is liberating

and I invite everyone

on this journey

of reflection and peace.

Loving humans

There is a certain type of love
that compels you to seek purpose;
run towards it do not look back.

Loving humans
comes with a made-up mind
to forgive and forget
as easily as you breathe.

I am compelled
to take that journey every day.

Bloom

I stand in awe
each time I see
a woman
who was once broken
in full bloom.

No flower
blooms overnight,
quality time
was spent in the dirt,
appreciate the bloom.

Restored

She said yes
countless times
when it should have been no.

She saw roses
in meadows full of thorns,
tears and woe.

She offered patience
peace and calm;
she lived in the future
not in the present.

She found her true self again;
it was in the midst
of a raging war.

The restored woman is free

to change her mind,

her direction,

her whole life,

with that freedom

she will always choose the things

that nurture her soul.

Heal

I have seen broken women
who cannot find peace
they pursue drama not healing.

Broken woman
you have nothing to prove,
your pain is your own
the world also grieves.

Woman
your heart bleeds,
heal.

I remember

I remember the day
my heart spoke lingering words of change,
the sun rose for me,
I remember the day.

I remember the day
my heart moved from darkness and gloom;
all this time I was growing
tears watered my hopes to full bloom.

I remember the day
my heart found time,
time mistaken for a tomb,
each chamber flung wide open,
I found solitude.

Breathe

As you begin to rise
be prepared to welcome
a shift in temperature.

Altitude changes
can be frightening;
nature itself signals change
through seasons and cycles.

Be still
breathe

Invaluable

Her value never diminishes
no matter the company;
she is never concerned
with impressing the crowd.

Her vision is clear,
her calling is higher,
she pursues purpose
never seeking the companionship of luck.

Her value can never be quantified
by imperfect human effort,
there lies her worth it is divine.

Tribe

The woman who walks in purpose
finds no joy in boasting,
gloating or undermining.
She is eager to admire,
encourage,
celebrate and inspire.

Every day she takes a moment
to connect with her tribe,
she shares visions, goals,
ambitions, fears, disappointments
and her faith.
She knows her tribe.

Dove

When a dove descends
to your window sill
seeking shelter
from the uncertainties of the world,
let it in.

When it bows its head and coos
listen with your heart
it is a song from the depth of its soul;
respond with likewise fervour
holding nothing back.

Give unto it what it seeks,
the gentleness and kindness of a child,
whose most malicious thought
is to love unconditionally.

Give unto it the emotions it cherishes;
it will fuel unfathomable joy.
The cycle will be completed
when the essence of the soul
is manifested in truth.

Love

Love found her
in the most unexpected way,
it found her
and she was not blown away.

It whispered in her ear
and her insecurities were gone,
it took each one
and ripped it apart.

Love touched her
igniting flames of passion
from the inside;
it consumed
the broken walls of pain
leaving no doubt behind.

It moved her,
quieted the voices of suspicion,
it taught her to listen to her own soul.

Love healed her

it opened her heart;

it crawled under her skin

removing every remnant of scars.

It found her and taught her to believe.

The smile in her eyes returned,

she felt strong,

she felt free.

Live

Live life in its true colours.

Laugh deafeningly

at the jokes

only you understand.

Speak less of the nonsense

others treasure,

your soul knows fire.

Ignore those

that seek to censor you,

they have insecurities to hide.

Let each day

find you in purpose,

new exploits

in spaces for growth.

Your authenticity

will aggravate the pretentious

but your soul will always be free.

The gift

Your pain was a gift
you accepted unwillingly
thinking by it
you would have been reduced.

Your pain was a gift
an unwelcome fiend;
your plans put before the divine
were never discarded.

Your pain was a gift
it broadened your walls,
solitude is now a friend.

Your pain was a gift
one you did not choose
but you made it your tool.

Storm

I fell in love with the storm
never thought I would feel this way;
she spoke to me in so many ways.

I was captivated by her beauty,
her strength, her aura,
her flair.
I loved the way
she refused to hide her tears.

She unleashes her fury,
pummelling mountains
while bursting through streams.
She rips through valleys;
listen to the wind you will hear.

She clears her own path
leaving nothing to time,
only shreds of memories
are left behind.

I fell in love with the storm;

I fell in love with her pain.

I fell in love

with the way

she lets you know

she passed this way.

Sacred journey

My journey is sacred,

I refuse to carry

that which seeks to pollute my soul.

Tuned out the senseless chatter,

endured ridicule,

knowing fully well

I will be misunderstood.

My conscience

will not be burdened

with unrighteous bonds

that suffocate me.

I refuse to reconcile with demons

prancing in robes of treachery,

proclaiming the message of humility and peace

while injecting hate and bitterness

beneath my skin.

My journey is sacred
nothing happens by chance;
I embrace the vision
knowing it is time.

My journey is sacred
it cannot be taken in haste.
I now walk along the trail,
abandoning the open road,
carefully
choosing my path.

Dreams

Dreams

are not meant to be forgotten

or hidden behind windows of despair.

They are meant to be strands of hope

when life itself

it seems you cannot bear.

In essence

dreams are meaningful

and keep a person whole.

Neglecting its true meaning

will often make one as cold

as the ice that was,

which melts

and slithers down your glass.

So will the future you once had

dissipate into the past.

Dawn

115

My thoughts rise with the sun, my most pressing question, are you ready to honour the dream?

Twenty-four hours

The sun leisurely rises,
mother nature meticulously
orchestrating her way.

Feeling warmth,
in sync with the music,
joy returned
on swift happy feet.

I've done one hundred hours
of this twenty-four-hour day.

Diamond mind

These feet have walked miles
through countless oil fields,
searching for wealth,
chasing a dream.

These eyes have peered longingly
at abandoned coal mines thinking,
all hope was lost
with the passage of time.

These hands combed deserts
eager to unearth gold,
salt ponds and seashells
were the best finds.

This heart found solace
no more longing for home.
I found a diamond mind
my heart is home.

Home

Home,
the way it was,
the way things are
the way they will be.

The purge

I set the museum on fire;
I refuse to bury the bones.
I smile,
the heap of ashes
now lies cold.

I set the museum on fire;
every precious exhibit removed.

All that's left are memories,
no need to build a tomb.

I set the museum on fire
though fastened by rusty chains.
Diamonds never fear the heat,
the conflagration rose up like a beast
and devoured my jail.

Memories of my pain

The memories of my pain
I left in the fields,
buried deep inside the earth
where my ancestors sleep.

The memories of my pain
were scattered in the Nile,
every bit swallowed up.
I bowed my head
and smiled.

The memories of my pain
float in the dead sea.
Who could have imagined that?
Ah child, I am free!

Shovelling sand

The task of shovelling sand
to the uninspired man
is absurd,
it's a futile task he says.

Look to the inspired man,
he can withstand misrepresentations
when his strengths are condemned as vices
by the juror's haste.

Shovelling sand with intention
takes great care,
clear vision,
only a true builder
can envision its outcome.

Shovelling sand is sacrifice,
if overdone it leads to demise,
if done with care
empires rise for years to come.

The legacy is told
not when the shovel picks up its load,
shovelling sand is an act of service
the future knows.

The man who shovels sand
bows his head
and doesn't glance,
when met with disappointment
he turns his back to the wind.

The trail of legacy
never follows those who only speak,
keep shovelling sand
you have more empires left to build.

Wages

I have no plans for tomorrow;
if I wait,
I'll die of thirst.
Today my cup of gratitude rises,
my heart full,
barefoot I walk the earth.

I'll give again a hundred,
a thousand
without gifts from the multitude's lips.
This act of service is timeless,
its intent
the fool and the reckless will miss.

The ocean is restless,
it rises,
yet daily we beg for rain.
I have no plans for tomorrow;
I earn full wages today.

Nirvana bay

I sat on the boat roaming the seas,

rain clouds came along,

the thunder greeted me.

Each nostalgic wave

came and left me in a daze,

now stuck on the sand bank

I must wait.

Reflecting on how I sailed off

on this optimistic boat,

dreams of chasing the horizon slowed.

A lesson I must learn,

this monster of a sand bank

provides an unexpected turn.

Must I stay here and weep?

Oh no!

On the sandbank I'll stay,
I can enjoy the view
maybe all day or
I can frustrate my weary heart
with intents to explore.

For a moment I had to decide
to put my heartache aside
and wave to those passing,
lighten the weight.

It was a beautiful day,
sights and sounds I saved.
Why did I plan to race by Nirvana Bay?

Summoned

My soul summoned me to silence;

I am not lost the temple changed.

Exchanged rags for robes,

beating heart be still.

My soul summoned me to listen

to the stillness inside;

I close my eyes

there is nothing to hide.

My soul summoned me to visions,

visions I thought had long escaped.

The one key I thought was useless

now opens this monstrous gate.

My soul summoned me to the valleys

to which I once eloped.

I sighed, I was blind,

I was naked,

the forest gifted me a cloak.

My soul summoned me to the music,

music of hearts pulsating with hope.

The mountain stretched her arms wide open

and yes,

I am ready,

I must go.

Miles to go

My humility grows

when I look back on how far I have come,

optimism climbs

thinking of the mountains conquered.

My gratitude soars

knowing

I was never alone,

eagerness multiplied

seeing there are more miles to go.

Hot sand

129

She has felt the hot sand
between her toes,
she did her time
on the threshing floor.

Her heart has been broken
and mended,
she now builds bridges not doors.

Threshold

She stands on the threshold of greatness,
she has come a very long way.
Her path was rugged and treacherous,
she is ready
to honour the dream.

Her character has been fortified,
she will not be daunted by her past,
her vision
will inspire the world
a creator of new dreams.

Emergence

I am standing in a place
I have never been before;
the air is tranquil,
the untainted river runs low.

The ones in the distance
beckon me,
I think about my life
and each tragedy.

I learnt from the river
to walk in a divinely set path;
bridges must be built
do not cherish wrath.

Like that river
I am unstoppable;
each season
I am renewed.

My mind made up,

woman you have nothing

to lose.

This is my dawn

it is where I must be.

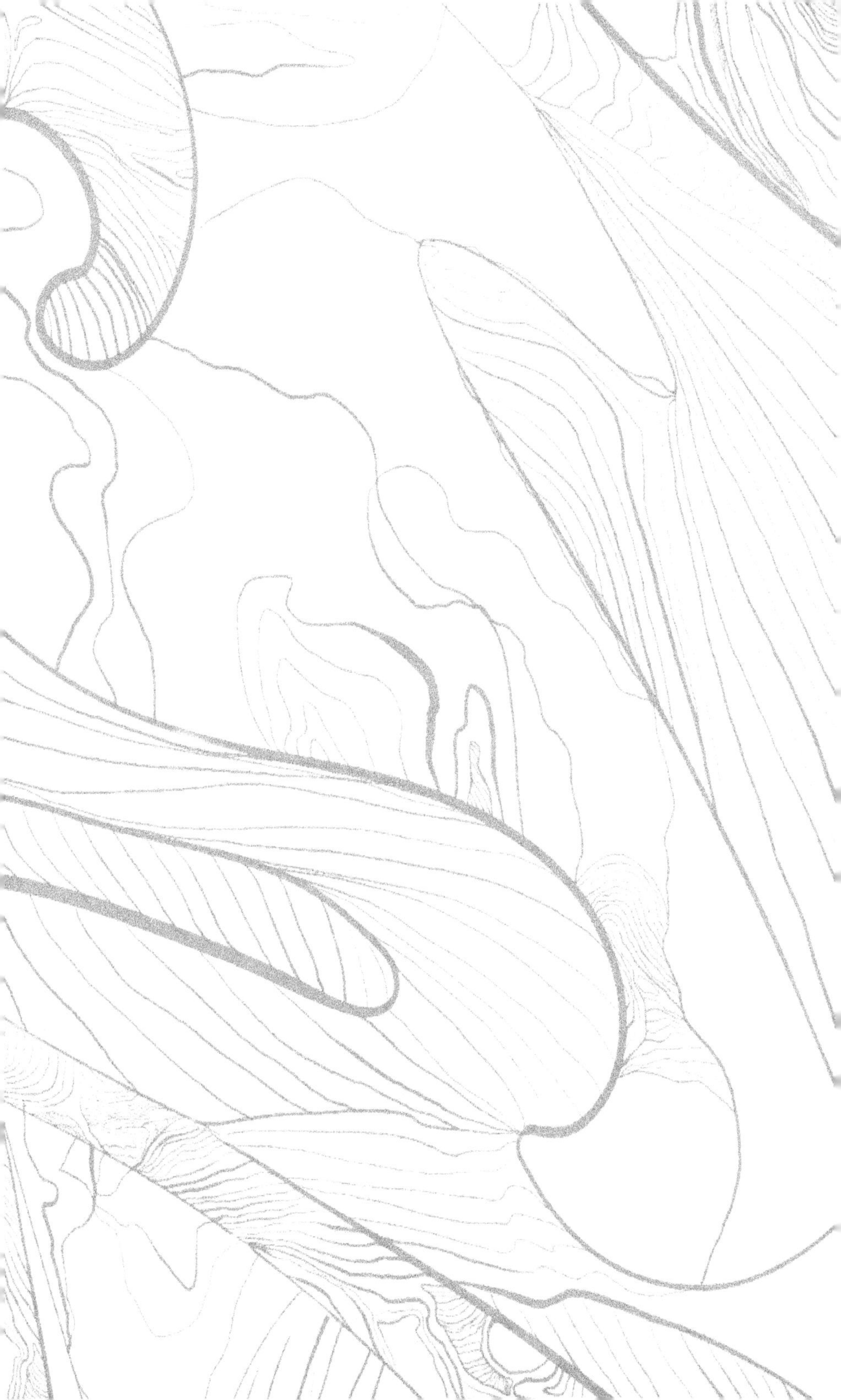

About the Author

Stacie Ann is a Jamaican woman who enjoys writing about the human experience. Her passion for writing was born out of a desire to inspire others to own their journey and live courageously. She shares her deepest emotions and thoughts about life in her debut poetry book *I Found my Heart*.

To connect with the author, you can do so via the following social media handles:

- Twitter @stacieanapoetry
- Facebook @stacieanapoetry
- Instagram @stacieanapoetry

www.ingramcontent.com/pod-product-compliance
Lightning Source LLC
Chambersburg PA
CBHW072333150726
47998CB00017B/529